Hearing the Voice
of the Spirit

VOLUME 4

Hearing *the* Voice *of the* Spirit

*The Spirit came into me as he spoke
and set me on my feet. I listened
carefully to his words. Ezekiel 2:2*

....

A 30-day Devotional Bible Study
for Individuals or Groups.

....

Dr. Larry Keefauver

CREATION
H O U S E
Orlando, FL

Hearing the Voice of the Spirit by Larry Keefauver

Published by Creation House
Strang Communications Company
600 Rinehart Road
Lake Mary, FL 32746

Web site: http://www.creationhouse.com

Unless otherwise noted, all Scripture quotations are the Holy Bible, New Living Translation, copyright © 1996. Used by permission of Tyndale House Publishers, Inc., Wheaton, IL 60189. All rights reserved.

ISBN 0-88419-473-6

78901234 87654321

Contents

Introduction

Welcome to this devotional study on *Hearing the Voice of the Spirit* that will assist you in welcoming the Holy Spirit into your life. This is one of eight devotional study guides related to the *Holy Spirit Encounter Bible*. Though not absolutely necessary, it is recommended that you obtain a copy of the *Holy Spirit Encounter Bible* for your personal use with this study guide. We make this recommendation because the same translation used in this guide, the *New Living Translation*, is also used in the *Holy Spirit Encounter Bible*.

It is also recommended that you choose the study guides in this series in the sequence that best meets your spiritual needs. So please don't feel that you must go through them in any particular order. Each study guide has been developed for individual, group, or class use.

Additional instruction has been included at the end of this guide for those desiring to use it in class or group settings.

Because the purpose of this guide is to help readers encounter the person of the Holy Spirit through the Scriptures, individuals going through it are invited to use it for personal daily devotional reading and study. Each daily devotional is structured to:

❖ Probe deeply into the Scriptures.

❖ Examine one's own personal relationship with the Holy Spirit.

❖ Discover biblical truths about the Holy Spirit.

❖ And, encounter the Person of the Holy Spirit continually in one's daily walk with God.

It is our prayer as you encounter the voice of the Holy Spirit in this devotional study that you will learn to both hear and obey God so your heart will never be hardened (Heb. 4:7).

*A*nd I heard a voice from heaven saying, "Write this down: Blessed are those who die in the Lord from now on. Yes, says the Spirit, they are blessed indeed, for they will rest form all their toils and trials; for their good deeds follow them!" (Rev. 14:13).

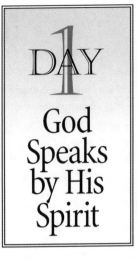

DAY 1

God Speaks by His Spirit

You're probably familiar with the subject of *the voice of God*, because God has spoken to His people through various means since greeting Adam in the garden. So this study will explore how God's voice is heard through the person of the Holy Spirit.

But because what we believe about the Holy Spirit is a key to what He will do in our lives, let's first ask if you believe that God's Spirit still speaks today as He did in Scripture through the prophets and Christ (Heb. 1:1–3, 2:1–4). Circle one of the following responses: (SA–Strongly agree; A–agree; U–undecided; D–disagree; SD–strongly disagree) to the following statements:

SA   A   U   D   SD   1. God's Spirit speaks today through us to others as He did through His prophets of old.

SA   A   U   D   SD   2. The voice of the Holy Spirit is verified today by signs and wonders.

SA   A   U   D   SD   3. The Spirit's voice may be heard through my language or His language.

SA   A   U   D   SD   4. The Spirit's voice teaches, counsels, warns, advises, and directs us.

In the studies that follow, you will discover in Scripture how the Spirit's voice does everything listed above. If you haven't experienced hearing the Spirit's voice, then get ready now to let the Word teach you how to listen and receive.

Revelation 14:13 says, *Yes, says the Spirit, they are blessed indeed.* So it is clear from this verse that the Spirit does speak, and that God's Word actually does quote what the Spirit has said. Read the following scriptures, then jot down some of the ways the Spirit spoke to God's prophets and apostles in Scripture:

Isaiah 48:16 _____

Ezekiel 3:24 _____

Ezekiel 11:2, 5 _____

Zechariah 7:12_____

Acts 4:8 _____

Acts 8:29 _____

Acts 10:19 _____

Acts 13:2 _____

In the coming days, you will discover that when the Holy Spirit speaks, He both directs and empowers your life.

> *God uses the indwelling Holy Spirit to speak His Word and will into your heart.*

So listen, obey, and don't harden your heart.

Ask Yourself . . .

❖ When was the last time you heard the Spirit's voice speak to your heart?

❖ What is the Spirit speaking into your life right now?

Write a prayer asking God's Spirit to begin speaking into your life whenever He desires:

_____

_____

_____

_____

_____

*T*he Holy Spirit told me to go with them and not to worry about their being Gentiles (Acts 11:12).

DAY 2
The Spirit's Voice Directs

The Holy Spirit will speak to your heart and direct your paths. Acts 11:12 says the Spirit's voice told Peter what to do and instructed him not to worry. Has the Holy Spirit ever been that direct with you?

The Holy Spirit really does want to tell you what to do. He has many different ways to direct you. So in the coming weeks, we will examine many of them in detail. But today let's focus on the Holy Spirit's primary method—His inspired Word (2 Tim. 3:16). The Spirit will use God's Word as a lamp to your feet and guide to your path (Ps. 119:105). Also remember from our study verse that the Spirit told Peter not to worry. Do you want His thoughts? Don't worry, read His Word. Facing a decision? Don't worry, read His Word.

What are the different situations you are facing now in which you need to hear the directing voice of God's Spirit through the Word:

_____

_____

_____

> The Spirit's voice never tells us to do something that contradicts God's Word.

One way to confirm when the Spirit is speaking is to compare what your thoughts are saying with God's Word (1 John 4:1). And never forget that throughout Scripture we are told, as was Peter, not to worry (Matt. 6:25–34; Phil. 4:6–7).

The Spirit's voice is also confirmed in various other ways. Below is a list of the other ways His voice can be verified. Check any you have experienced in the past:

❑ The Spirit in us gives witness to the truth (John 16:3).

❑ The Spirit's voice declares Jesus as God's Son, who came as a human being (1 John 4:2).

❑ There is unity among believers when the Spirit speaks (Eph. 4:4).

❑ Agreement exists between the Holy Spirit and the fellowship of the saints (Acts 15:28).

❑ The Spirit's voice brings peace to your mind (Rom. 8:6).

❑ The Spirit's voice turns us from legalism—the sinful nature and its evil deeds (Rom. 8:13).

❑ What the Spirit's voice tells us to do is rooted in God's (*agape*) love (Rom. 15:30; 1 Cor. 13)

❑ His voice is confirmed by many witnesses (2 Tim. 2:2).

❑ His voice is verified by signs and wonders (Heb. 2:4).

❑ The Word of God and the Spirit's voice agree (1 John 5:7; 2 Tim. 3:16–17).

God's Spirit does, and will, speak to you. But not every spiritual voice you hear comes from the Holy Spirit. So God has given us many ways to hear, receive, and confirm the Spirit's voice.

As with Elijah (1 Kings 19:12–13), God's voice comes to us as a gentle whisper. So listen closely. It will only be when every other competing voice is silenced from within and without you that you will be able to prayfully hear the voice of the Holy Spirit.

Ask Yourself . . .

❖ What is the Spirit telling you to do?

❖ How does the Spirit of God want you to respond to what He has been saying in your heart?

Write a prayer asking God's Spirit to silence every competing voice in your life so you can clearly hear Him:

_____

_____

_____

_____

*T*hen the Spirit said to me, "Son of man, these are the men who are responsible for the wicked counsel being given in this city" (Ezek.11:2).

The Holy Spirit will speak revelation to us about things we would have otherwise never known. The Spirit lifted Ezekiel up over the East Gate of the Temple and revealed to him twenty-five prominent men who were giving wicked counsel. This word of knowledge came to Ezekiel by the voice of the Spirit. It was important revelation that affected the people of God. Do you desire this kind of revelation from the Holy Spirit?

We can't discover God's will in our own strength. But God's Spirit will seek us out to reveal whatever God wants us to know. Jesus said, "All that the Father has is mine; this is what I mean when I say that the Spirit will reveal to you whatever he receives from me" (John 16:15).

> *All the Father wants us to know He has spoken to the Word—Jesus Christ. All the Son wants us to know—He says to the Holy Spirit. Then all the Spirit wants us to know—He reveals to our born-again hearts.*

Of course we may never know all there is to know about God. But what we *need* to know, God has given to the Son, who gives to His Spirit, to reveal to us. The Holy Spirit inspired the written Word of God so God's plan of eternal salvation could be revealed to us in Christ. Read Ephesians 1:3–14, then summarize this mystery that God has revealed to us:

_____

_____

But for every spiritual truth, there is a counterfeit. That's why some people major in minors. They dabble in religious mysticism that pretends to be special revelation given only to a few. Paul wrote about such false teachings in Colossians 2; 2 Timothy 3; and 2 Thessalonians 2. There is revelation from the Spirit that speaks clearly and directs us to obey His Word. But there is also speculation. So below is a list of some things we need to know as Spirit-led believers, and some things we don't. Check what you believe are the essentials:

❏ How to be saved.

❏ The exact day and time of Jesus' return.

- ❏ How to witness.
- ❏ How to be sanctified by the Holy Spirit.
- ❏ How to minister to others.
- ❏ What happens every moment in heaven.
- ❏ How to have a strong Christian home, marriage, and family.
- ❏ Special techniques and styles for worship.
- ❏ How to contact spirits.
- ❏ Special holy days and ceremonies.
- ❏ How to do good, love mercy, and walk humbly before God.

Salvation, evangelism, sanctification, servanthood, Christian relationship, and living a humble life are essential to our Christian walk. While we may be curious about other issues, it is dangerous to focus any attention and time on them that would be better spent in the Word, in worship and prayer, and listening to the Spirit's voice.

Ezekiel spent time in God's presence listening to the Spirit, and the Holy Spirit spoke. Are you ready to hear the essential things of the Spirit that aren't religious and speculative ideas?

Ask Yourself

❖ How is the Spirit revealing truth from His mind to you?

❖ What religious things distract you from hearing His voice?

Write a prayer asking Jesus to send His Spirit to reveal a word of knowledge concerning something He wants you to know:

_____

_____

_____

_____

_____

*A*s for Philip, an angel of the Lord said to him, "Go south down the desert road that runs from Jerusalem to Gaza." The Holy Spirit said to Philip, "Go over and walk along beside the carriage." (Acts 8:26, 29) But when the Holy Spirit has come upon you, you will receive power and will tell people about me everywhere (Acts 1:8).

DAY 4

His Voice Sends

An Ethiopian eunuch needed Christ. One lost from the Father needed to be found. So the Spirit of God sought Him out to redeem him in a very powerful way, just as He wants to send us to witness in His powerful way (Acts 1:8).

> *The Spirit is continually speaking to us about someone who needs Christ.*

Sometimes we plead with God to tell us what He wants us to do and to show us where He wants us to go. But if we listen very closely, we may hear him whispering to us as He did to Philip, "Go over and walk along beside the lost. Lead them to Jesus."

Read each of the following stories, then summarize after each how God sent His servants to win the lost:

Isaiah was sent . . .   Isaiah's response to God was . . .

(Isaiah 6:1–8)   _____

                            _____

The disciples were sent . . .   The disciples response to God was . . .

(Luke 9:1–6)   _____

                            _____

Peter was sent . . .   Peter's response to God was . . .

(Acts 11:10–14)   _____

                            _____

Do you notice a pattern here? The Spirit of God wants us to share His Word with others. He sends. We obey.

Some believers wait a long time hoping to hear the Spirit's voice tell them what to do. And they still miss the Spirit's GO! What keeps you from obeying His voice and going to the lost? Circle anything that hinders you:

Fear	Ignorance	Busyness
Insecurity	Unbelief	Other:_____

The Holy Spirit empowered Philip to discern the Ethiopian's spiritual condition, to share and explain the Gospel, then to lead the man to Christ. What the Holy Spirit did for Philip, He will also do for you.

The voice of the Holy Spirit speaks to you the same words Jesus spoke in Matthew 28:19. So fill in the blank of your own special call to fulfill the great commission:

_____, *therefore, go and make disciples of all*
(Your name)

the nations _____
(List two or more people you need to witness to.)

baptizing them in the name of the Father and the Son

and the Holy Spirit (Matt. 28:19).

Ask Yourself . . .

❖ To whom is the Spirit sending you for the purpose of sharing the Gospel?

❖ What keeps you from hearing the Spirit's voice when He tells you to *Go!*

Write a prayer asking God's Spirit to show you to whom you need to go:

_____

_____

_____

*T*he voice spoke again, "If God says something is acceptable, don't say it isn't . . ." Meanwhile, as Peter was puzzling over the vision, the Holy Spirit said to him, "Three men have come looking for you. Go down and go with them without hesitation. All is well, for I have sent them" (Acts 10:15, 19).

DAY 5
His Voice Interprets

The Holy Spirit dispels confusion and will interpret the meaning of what's happening within and around us. As our counselor (John 14:16), the Spirit's voice will explain any situation or relationship that perplexes us.

Notice that the Spirit spoke during the vision that He revealed to Peter. First he gave the vision, then He interpreted it.

> *No one can truly know what a dream or vision from God means except by the Spirit of God.*

Some important truths regarding how the Spirit interprets truth are also revealed in Pharoah's account. In Genesis 41, Pharaoh received two dreams, and puzzled over what they meant. So read Genesis 41, then complete these sentences:

Both the dreams and their interpretation came from _____
_____.

Joseph was told the meaning of the dreams by _____
_____.

Once Pharaoh understood the interpretation, his responsibility was to _____
_____.

The same truths can be found in Peter's story contained in Acts 10. Here is the process of interpretation that the Spirit uses:

1. The Holy Spirit inspires dreams and visions (Acts 2:17).
2. Those receiving His revelations may not understand their meaning.
3. The Holy Spirit interprets His dreams and visions.
4. The Holy Spirit tells those given His dreams and visions what to say and do.
5. Once His interpretation is given, obedience must follow.

The Holy Spirit	➡	Gives dreams and visions
The voice of the Spirit	➡	Speaks an interpretation
The indwelling Spirit	➡	Empowers us to obey

Describe a time in your life when . . .

1. The Holy Spirit gave you a dream or vision:

_____

_____

2. The Spirit interpreted the dream or vision to mean:

_____

_____

3. The Spirit empowered you in obedience to:

_____

_____

Ask Yourself . . .

❖ What vision or dream has the Spirit inspired in your life for the future?

❖ What do you hear the Spirit's voice telling you to do?

Write a prayer asking God's Spirit to speak His interpretation into your life whenever you are puzzled:

_____

_____

_____

_____

_____

*O*ne day as these men were worshiping the Lord and fasting, the Holy Spirit said, "Dedicate Barnabas and Saul for the special work I have for them" (Acts 13:2).

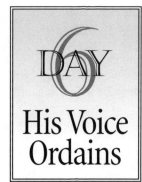

DAY 6

His Voice Ordains

To accomplish anything for God, we must first be chosen and ordained for His mission. His mission for us may be a simple task that can be completed in a moment. Or it could be a complicated, life-long ordeal.

Regardless, it is the Spirit's ordination that releases His power to accomplish His tasks. He chooses our mission—instead of us choosing the task, then asking for His blessing to go ahead on our own.

Think for a moment of some of the tasks, projects or missions you're doing right now and evaluate how they're going. First write out the task, then place a check by each one indicating whether you think it is a good idea or a God idea. Then put an *x* in the column indicating how prosperous the task is.

Task	Good idea	God idea	It is . . .	
			Prospering	Failing
			Prospering	Failing
			Prospering	Failing
			Prospering	Failing

The ultimate acid test of ordination is good fruit. That's why Jesus said, "My true disciples produce much fruit. This brings great glory to my Father" (John 15:8).

So say this verse aloud, very deliberately:
"You didn't choose me [Jesus]. I chose you. I appointed you to go and produce fruit that will last, so that the Father will give you whatever you ask for, using my name. I command you to love each other" (John 15:16–17).

> When Jesus sends His Spirit to ordain or appoint you for a particular mission, He guarantees in His name both the power to go and the strength to complete it.

The Spirit also speaks to other believers surrounding you concerning His call on your life. When this happens they may confirm your call by the laying on of hands and prayer.

Read the following scriptures, then jot down what they say about being chosen, appointed, and ordained for the work of God:

Exodus 28:41; 29:9, 35 _____

Mark 3:14 _____

Acts 6:6, 14:23, 16:4 _____

Hebrews 5:1_____

When the Spirit's voice ordains, He speaks . . .

> ❖ The purpose of His mission.
> ❖ To those who are to pray and support.
> ❖ The time to start and to complete.
> ❖ The direction He desires you to go.
> ❖ To the hearts of other believers confirming your mission.
> ❖ The power into your life to accomplish His mission.
> ❖ Assurance into your heart to persevere and finish strong in the Spirit.

Has the Spirit's voice spoken to you about a mission you are ordained to accomplish? If so, circle all of the above statements that have already taken place or are currently happening in your spiritual walk. Then underline those that still need to happen. Finally, give God glory for all He is doing, and repent (if you need to) of anything you are trying to do to make something happen.

Ask Yourself . . .

❖ What are you doing that the Spirit has spoken to and ordained you to do?

❖ What do you need to stop doing that is a good idea but not a God idea?

Write a prayer thanking God's Spirit for one thing He has ordained and consecrated you to do:

_____

_____

_____

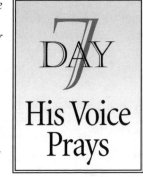

DAY 7

His Voice Prays

*A*nd the Holy Spirit helps us in our distress. For we don't even know what we should pray for, nor how we should pray. But the Holy Spirit prays for us with groanings that cannot be expressed in words (Rom. 8:26).

There are times when we know we need to pray but the words simply won't come. We desire prayer, but we have no idea of how or what to pray. It is at those times that the Spirit of God prays for us, in us, through us, and sometimes—in spite of us.

When you know you need to pray, but can't find the words, how do you feel? Cross out every feeling you don't have at such a time:

Confidence	Boldness	Weakness
Strength	Power	Determination
Peace	Depressed	Understanding
Confused	Puzzled	Perplexed

You probably crossed out the positive confident feelings in this exercise and left the negative, doubt-filled feelings uncrossed. Why? Because when we can't pray, the enemy uses every negative feeling we have to keep us from yielding to the voice of the Spirit who wants to pray in, for, and through us.

So now complete these sentences:

One thing I feel distressed about and can't seem to find a way to pray about is

_____.

The negative feelings I need to release are _____

_____.

For the Spirit's voice to pray through me, I must yield to _____

_____.

When the Spirit prays for us *with groanings that cannot be expressed with words,* we are praying beyond words.

> *Intercession is not so much that we are laying our burdens on God, it is God burdening us to pray for whatever He desires to accomplish.*

"God blesses those who mourn, for they shall be comforted" (Matt. 5:4). One paraphrase of this verse might be: *Blessed are those who are brokenhearted by the things that break God's heart.* And the only prayer appropriate for some situations in life is the prayer that identifies with Jesus' sufferings (Gal. 6:17; Phil. 3:10–11).

Below are some ways we pray beyond words that need to be empowered by the voice of the Spirit. Put in rank order the frequency with which the Spirit prays through you from 1 (most frequent), to 7 (least frequent).

_____ Through groanings

_____ Through silence

_____ Through praying in unknown tongues

_____ Through tears

_____ Through laughter or inexpressible joy

_____ Through awe

_____ Through _____

What keeps you from allowing the voice of the Spirit to pray for, and through you?_____

_____

Ask Yourself . . .

❖ Under what circumstances does the Spirit pray through you with intercession beyond words?

❖ Are you fully yielded to His voice in your prayer life?

Sit silently and quietly, praying in the Spirit—beyond human words.

B *ut I will send you the Counselor—the Spirit of truth. He will come to you from the Father and will tell you all about me (John 15:26).*

Jesus describes the Holy Spirit with the word, *paraclete*, which means, "to stand along side." Imagine two close friends walking arm-in-arm, side-by-side, down a road. There is virtually no daylight between them. They talk about everything and share every emotion as one person. In fact, they're so close they can simply whisper every word.

> *We never want to run ahead of the Holy Spirit, nor do we want to resist His leading and fall behind.*

The Paraclete comes along side of every decision we make and breathes the Word of God into our minds teaching us what to think, say, and do. The Holy Spirit speaks into our lives the nature and character of Christ.

Below are some of Christ's qualities that the Spirit speaks into our lives. Match the quality listed to the verse describing it, then circle those qualities you need most today for the decisions you face in life. Draw a line from each quality to its correct text:

Christ-like Qualities	Texts
Isaiah 40:13	Grace and prayer
Isaiah 42:1	New Life
Isaiah 11:2	Love
Zechariah 12:10	Justice
John 16:13	Holiness
Romans 5:5	Fear of God
Romans 8:2	Teaching
Romans 14:17	Peace and Joy
2 Corinthians 6:6	Unity
Galatians 5:16	True life
Ephesians 4:3	Truth
1 Peter 1:2	Purity

The Holy Spirit wants to transform you from glory into glory into the image of Christ (2 Cor. 3:18). So He speaks Christ's life into your life continually. He advises you in right from wrong decisions by convicting the choice you are considering with the nature of Christ. Then He directs you to make the right choice because it conforms to His nature.

Not only will the Holy Spirit *give* you righteous counsel, He will also give you the power to *act* upon His counsel. We may be told what is right by our lower sinful nature, but we are powerless to do it. In the Spirit, however, we have the power not only to hear, but to make right choices and to do the right thing.

Describe a time when the Holy Spirit counseled you in making a decision, then gave you the power to do what He said:

_____

_____

Ask Yourself . . .

❖ What decision are you presently facing that the Holy Spirit is counseling you about?

❖ How well do you receive and obey the counsel of the Spirit?

Write a prayer asking the Holy Spirit to give you wise counsel in every decision you make:

_____

_____

_____

_____

_____

*W*hen the Father sends the Counselor as my representative—and by the Counselor I mean the Holy Spirit—he will teach you everything and will remind you of everything I myself have told you. (John 14:26)

His Voice Teaches

The Spirit's voice will always remind us of the truth He inspired in the pages of God's Word. The Spirit is God's living reminder who prompts us with His Word, then increases our thirst for more.

Are you allowing the Holy Spirit to teach you the Word? Remember, He only brings to remembrance what you have taken the time to know.

> *If the Word isn't in you, then the Holy Spirit has nothing to remind you of!*

How do you get the Word of God in you? Below is a list of ways. Circle how often you have been consuming the meat of God's Word in each area:

I am feeding on the Word . . .

Through Bible reading

Daily	Weekly	Rarely	None

Through Bible study

Daily	Weekly	Rarely	None

Through memorizing Scripture

Daily	Weekly	Rarely	None

Through meditating on Scripture

Daily	Weekly	Rarely	None

Through praying Scripture

Daily	Weekly	Rarely	None

Through singing Scripture

Daily	Weekly	Rarely	None

The Holy Spirit teaches us both the meaning and the application of Scripture. He helps us understand which passages apply to specific situations in life. He may use ministry and spiritual gifts in the body such as teaching, the word of knowledge, prophecy, and the word of wisdom to get this done. As we receive His body gifts and exalt God in worship, we are built up in the Word and directed in our decisions.

Read Psalm 119:9–16 then check all the ways you respond to the Spirit's prompting in the Word:

❑ Obedience   ❑ Seeking His Word

❑ Hiding the Word in your heart   ❑ Fixed on His Word

❑ Reciting aloud the Word   ❑ Rejoicing

❑ Studying   ❑ Reflecting

❑ Not forgetting   ❑ Delighting

In what areas of your life do you need to be taught the Word of God? List three areas you want the Spirit to more fully instruct you (for example, relationships, friendships, work, marriage, finances, habits, or ministry):

1._____

2._____

3._____

Ask Yourself . . .

❖ Are you getting the Word into your heart so the Spirit has something there to bring to your remembrance?

❖ How do you need to increase your feeding on God's Word?

Write a prayer asking the Spirit to fill you with His inspired hunger to study and understand the Word:

_____

_____

_____

_____

_____

A nd when he [the Holy Spirit] comes, he will convince the world of its sin, and of God's righteousness, and of the coming judgment (John 16:8).

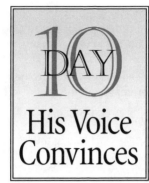

When the Spirit convinces the world of sin, He confronts us with the reality that all have sinned and fallen short of God's perfect and holy standards (Rom. 3:23). Encountering His conviction is not always pleasant, but always necessary.

Why do we need the Holy Spirit to convince and convict us of sin? We fail to do so ourselves, because:

- ❖ *Sin addicts.* It denies there is a problem or that one is guilty.
- ❖ *Sin deceives.* It tries to make us believe our own lies.
- ❖ *Sin destroys.* It sears our conscience, judgment, and discernment.
- ❖ *Sin is habit forming.* The more we sin the easier it becomes to sin again.
- ❖ *Sin is pleasurable for the moment,* but produces a harvest of destruction and pain for a lifetime.

Look over the above list. Underline the quality of sin that has the strongest foothold in your life. Then ask the Holy Spirit to convict you as you answer these questions:

What sinful habit do you constantly deny? _____

_____.

What lie do you tell yourself most often? _____

_____.

What sinful pleasure are you presently engaged in that you know will bring you

long-term pain? _____

_____.

Where is your conscience seared? _____

_____.

Decide today to have a dialogue with the convincing, judging Holy Spirit. Do it right now.

> *The Holy Spirit will bring to the surface every hidden sin that is rendering you powerless.*

Ask the Father the following questions. Then listen to His Spirit's voice and write down His answers:

What television programs should I stop watching? _____

_____

What habit should I give up? _____

_____

What do I say that repeatedly hurts my spouse, children, or family?_____

_____

What desire do I have that I need to surrender? _____

_____

What am I doing wrong that I need to start doing for His glory with excellence?

_____

Who is lost that I need to tell about Jesus? _____

_____

Ask Yourself . . .

❖ Do you really listen when the Spirit convinces you of your sin?

❖ What sins are you judging in the lives of others that are also present in your own life?

Write a prayer asking the Holy Spirit to bring to light all the areas of darkness and sin in your life:

_____

_____

_____

_____

_____

*W*hen the Spirit of truth comes, he will guide you into all truth. He will not be presenting his own ideas; he will be telling you what he has heard. He will tell you about the future (John 16:13).

God's Spirit dwells in eternity and knows the end before the beginning, because time exists within Him and He is not confined by it. So the Holy Spirit knows our future and our destiny. We may not know what tomorrow holds, but we do know Him who holds tomorrow.

The Holy Spirit has revealed generally in His Word what your tomorrow in Christ will be like. Read each of the following Spirit-breathed passages to discover God's plan for your Christian future:

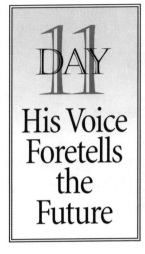

DAY 11

His Voice Foretells the Future

Your Future in Christ . . .

John 3:16 _____

Ephesians 1:9–14_____

Matthew 19:29 _____

Romans 6:23_____

2 Corinthians 5:1 _____

2 Timothy 2:10 _____

Romans 8:23_____

The Holy Spirit has revealed through the Word that our future in Christ is secure in eternity. But we also have assurance of God's blessings both for our temporal life today and tomorrow.

What does the Spirit's voice say to us about tomorrow with both its victories and its problems?

> *When we live in and listen to the Spirit in our todays, we can expect every promise of God to be fulfilled in our tomorrows.*

"But we who live by the Spirit eagerly wait to receive everything promised to us who are right with God through faith" (Gal. 5:5).

The Holy Spirit knows your long and short-term future in Christ. What biblical promises has the voice of the Spirit sealed within you for the coming weeks, months, and years? Complete these sentences:

For my family, God's Spirit has promised future _____

_____.

For my finances, God's Spirit has promised future _____

_____.

For my ministry serving others, God's Spirit has promised future _____

_____.

What other promises about the future has God's Spirit spoken to you? _____

_____.

When you encounter difficult circumstances, what is your usual response? Circle all that apply:

Worry	Disappointment	Lose faith
Feel angry	Become hopeless	Cry
Stay bold	Stand firm	Feel confident

Other: _____

When things get tough, those who listen to God's Spirit grow tougher, surer, more confident, and bolder. Why? Because they listen to the Spirit's voice about the future and refuse to give any attention to Satan's lies or the doomsayers.

Ask Yourself . . .

❖ When facing imminent future peril, to whom do you listen?

❖ What is the Spirit speaking to you about your future that fills you with excitement and hope?

Write a prayer thanking the Spirit of God for a victorious future as you live in Him:

_____

_____

*H*e [the Spirit] will bring me [Jesus] glory by revealing to you whatever he receives from me. All that the Father has is mine; this is what I mean when I say that the Spirit will reveal to you whatever he receives from me (John 16:14–15).

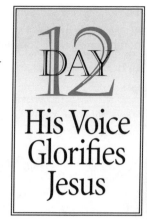

DAY 12

His Voice Glorifies Jesus

Glory is the honor, recognition, and praise due only to God for what He has done. The tendency of our human pride is to blame God, others, or the devil when things go wrong, but to take any credit and recognition when things go right.

Who gets the credit for success and prosperity in your life? Who do you blame when failure and sin surround you? Complete the following survey:

When I succeed financially, I praise _____.

When I have financial problems, I blame _____.

When my ideas work, I praise _____.

When my efforts fail, I blame _____.

I glorify God when He _____.

If you found yourself completing the last sentence without giving it more thought, you may want to pause a moment to consider this: Praise is due God simply because *He is God!*

The Holy Spirit doesn't need a reason to praise or glorify God. Why? Because He is worthy of praise. So the Spirit inspires glory and praise in us for the Father and the Son.

> *The voice of the Holy Spirit is continually filled with glory for the Father and the Son.*

When we turn to listen to the Holy Spirit's voice, the immediate and unceasing response we hear is the praise and honor of God.

Let's explore how this works as we listen to the Spirit's voice. No matter what the subject, or when you turn to the Spirit, you will hear Him glorifying Christ.

Check the different areas of your life in which you now have problems and need to hear from the Spirit. Then make a commitment to begin giving glory to the Son to release His answers and joy into these areas of your life:

❑ Work	❑ Family
❑ Marriage	❑ Parents
❑ Friendship	❑ Children
❑ Finances	❑ Church
❑ Future	❑ Self-esteem
❑ Other: _____	

No matter what your need in life, turn to the Holy Spirit to begin hearing His voice. When you do, the first thing you will hear is the Spirit praising and glorifying the Son. Then allow His accolades to inspire praise in your spirit because your response should be the same as His. In everything, lift up your voice of praise glorifying Jesus Christ!

Ask Yourself . . .

❖ For what do you need to join the Holy Spirit in praising Christ?

❖ What is the greatest problem you face? When will you begin to follow the Spirit in glorifying Christ in the midst of it?

Write a prayer that glorifies Jesus Christ:

_____

_____

_____

_____

_____

*T*he Spirit came into me as he spoke and set me on my feet. I listened carefully to his words (Ezek. 2:2).

A few times as a child, I was playing while my father was trying to speak. In each instance, he could tell I was paying little attention to him. So suddenly, and without warning, Dad would take hold of the back of my shirt, lift me up to my feet, put his face right in my face, and say what he said again. Whenever Dad did that, he had my complete and undivided attention.

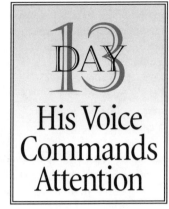

His Voice Commands Attention

The Spirit's voice so commanded Ezekiel's attention that he was lifted up bodily by the Holy Spirit to encounter the presence of God.

> *The Holy Spirit requires your undivided attention when He speaks.*

When the Spirit speaks, He demands that we stop everything we're doing to focus all our thoughts on what He is saying. Nothing should be allowed to distract us or hinder His voice.

But many things often do. Many voices compete for our attention. What voices in this world distract you from hearing His voice? Check any that apply:

❏ Bosses, employees, or customers

❏ Religious leaders

❏ Lusts and desires

❏ Television and radio

❏ Newspapers and magazines

❏ Family and friends

❏ Church members

❏ Others: _____

We are surrounded by voices constantly that compete to get our attention for the purposes of convincing us to buy, sell, go, or stay put. When the Spirit spoke to Ezekiel, He physically moved him from where he was to where the

Spirit wanted Him to be. In other words, the Holy Spirit removed Ezekiel from every distraction and other voice to a place where Ezekiel could give his undivided attention to God's voice and plan.

When do you give undivided attention to His voice? Rank in order of priority from 1 (most often), to 7 (least often), the time when the Spirit's voice has your undivided attention.

_____ When you pray.

_____ When you study or read the Word.

_____ When you worship.

_____ When you praise and sing unto the Lord.

_____ When you are still before Him.

_____ When you listen to the preaching of the Word.

_____ When you _____.

When the Spirit spoke to Ezekiel, He lifted him up, set him on his feet, and took him to a place where Ezekiel could give Him his undivided attention (Ezek. 2:2; 3:12; 3:14; 3:24; 8:3; 11:1; 11:24). Are you willing to go to a Spirit-designated place where He has your undivided attention when He speaks?

Ask Yourself . . .

❖ What distractions from hearing His voice do you need to remove from your life?

❖ To what place is the Spirit leading you where you can give Him your undivided attention?

Write a prayer asking God's Spirit to help you reach the place where you can focus totally on His voice:

_____

_____

_____

_____

_____

*T*hen the Spirit of God came upon Zechariah son of Jehoiada the priest. He stood before the people and said, "This is what God says: Why do you disobey the Lord's commands so that you cannot prosper? You have abandoned the Lord, and now he has abandoned you!" (2 Chron. 24:20).

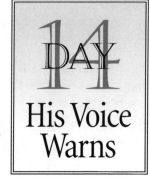

DAY 14

His Voice Warns

When a parent chooses, he or she can speak with a tone of voice that is filled with stern warning. The Spirit's voice can too. His voice warns us of the impending judgment of God and the consequences of our sins.

Throughout Israel's history, the Spirit's voice would come to various prophets warning Israel about the dire consequences of their sins. But Israel didn't heed the Spirit's voice, and was exiled to a foreign land.

How does the Spirit warn us of sin and God's judgment? Below is a list that shows how He does it through His people and in the pages of Scripture. Check all the ways you have heard Him warning you:

❑ Through the Word.

❑ Through prophecy.

❑ Through dreams and visions.

❑ Through events in history that He interprets.

❑ Through the love and concern of others among God's people.

❑ Through the gifts of the Spirit.

❑ Through preaching.

❑ Other: _____

The Spirit's voice warns to protect—not to frighten or intimidate.

> *God's Spirit speaks truth to us so we will know the consequences of continuing in sin and rebellion.*

God's Spirit issued both a solemn warning and a wonderful promise in 2 Chronicles 7:14. The words of His warning are written on the scroll below. Underline the part that warns, then circle the hopeful promise:

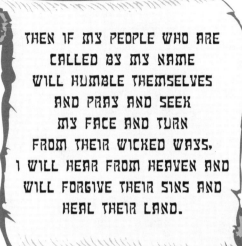

THEN IF MY PEOPLE WHO ARE
CALLED BY MY NAME
WILL HUMBLE THEMSELVES
AND PRAY AND SEEK
MY FACE AND TURN
FROM THEIR WICKED WAYS,
I WILL HEAR FROM HEAVEN AND
WILL FORGIVE THEIR SINS AND
HEAL THEIR LAND.

When you hear the warning of the Spirit's voice, do you heed it, turn from your sin, and seek God? Or, do you ignore His voice and rebel even further?

Ask Yourself . . .

❖ Is there any warning the Spirit's voice is speaking to you now? If so, how are you heeding that warning?

❖ When God's Spirit warns you in the future, what will be your immediate response?

Write a prayer thanking the Spirit for warning you of sin and destruction either in or around you:

_____

_____

_____

_____

_____

L *ook at my Servant, whom I have chosen. He is my Beloved, and I am very pleased with Him . . . I will put my Spirit upon him, and he will proclaim justice to the nations (Matt. 12:18; Isa. 42:1).*

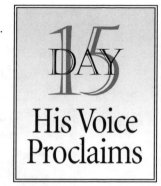

DAY 15

His Voice Proclaims

This proclamation in Isaiah and Matthew announced God's sending of His Messiah who would bring people into a just, or right, relationship with God. The Spirit spoke through the prophets and ultimately through Jesus to proclaim this truth to all people.

> *The Spirit-spoken proclamation of God's Word accomplishes powerful changes in our lives.*

When the anointing of God's Spirit came upon Jesus, the Messiah, many changes took place in people and in history itself. Isaiah 61 prophesied all the dramatic changes God would bring to pass when the Messiah fulfilled the Spirit's proclamation.

Below is a list of changes that happen as the result of the Spirit's proclamation that came through the anointed one of Israel. Match the change with the correct verse:

Changes Brought by Proclamation	Isaiah 61
Overwhelming joy	verse 3
Double portion of prosperity	verse 1
Reward for suffering	verse 3
Clothed in salvation and righteousness	verse 7
Praise instead of despair	verse 4
Release for captives	verse 8
Revival	verse 10
Beauty for ashes	verse 1
Comfort for the brokenhearted	verse 3

When the Holy Spirit anoints, or pours, Himself upon a person, the Spirit speaks through His mouthpiece with life-changing power. The proclamation of the Word comes forth with power to change and set people free from sin and bondage.

The Holy Spirit uses us as His voice in the world to proclaim God's message for all to hear. What are we to proclaim? Read each passage below, then jot down the good news of that proclamation:

Texts	Proclaim . . .
Deuteronomy 32:3	_____
1 Chronicles 16:8	_____
Psalm 50:6	_____
Psalm 71:15, 18	_____
Psalm 75:9	_____
Psalm 92:2	_____
Isaiah 25:9	_____
Amos 3:8	_____
Luke 4:18	_____
Galatians 1:16	_____
1 John 4:15	_____

We can become the vessels through whom the Spirit's voice speaks to proclaim God's good news to anyone who is lost, sick, in bondage, and hurting. The same gospel message that Jesus proclaimed is ours to announce to all who will listen. We have heard His voice. But are we willing to repeat His message to everyone we meet?

Ask Yourself . . .

❖ To whom is the Holy Spirit leading you to proclaim the good news of Jesus Christ?

❖ Through whom has the Spirit proclaimed good news to you?

Write a prayer thanking the Holy Spirit for all the saints through the ages who have proclaimed the good news:

_____

_____

_____

A ll Scripture is inspired by God and is useful to teach us what is true and to make us realize what is wrong in our lives. It straightens us out and teaches us to do what is right. It is God's way of preparing us in every way, fully equipped for every good thing God wants us to do (2 Tim. 3:16–17).

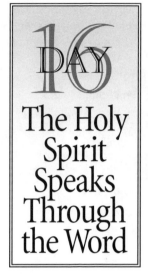

DAY 16
The Holy Spirit Speaks Through the Word

When Paul writes that, "all Scripture is *inspired of God*," he uses a powerful word—*theopneutos*. This literally means that God's Spirit has breathed into the written Word the very life and power of God. Scripture is more than words on a page describing the mighty acts of God in history.

> *The Holy Spirit speaks through Scripture to our minds and hearts.*

In our previous days of study and devotional reading we have explored many of the different *ways* the Holy Spirit speaks (prays, convicts, proclaims, teaches, counsels). In the second half of this study, we will discover the *means* through which the Spirit speaks. His voice is conveyed through various gifts of the Spirit and messages from the Spirit. But most of all, the Spirit speaks through Scripture inspired by the very breath of God.

Complete these sentences:

One way that the Spirit uses Scripture to speak to me is_____

_____.

I know that the Holy Spirit is speaking to me through Scripture when He _____

_____.

When I feed on His Word, the Spirit inspires me to_____

_____.

The Scripture is the sword of the Spirit (Eph. 6:17). So the Holy Spirit uses Scripture to cut through the superficial layers of our lives to surgically remove sin and iniquity. First, the Word convicts us of sin and teaches us how to confess and repent. Then, the Word provides God's promises for our healing and restoration after confession.

Read Hebrews 4:12, then paraphrase it in your own words:

_____

_____

The way the Spirit does surgery with the Word is described in 2 Timothy 3:16. As you encounter the Holy Spirit in the Word today, describe how He is speaking to your life. Complete each statement:

One thing the Spirit is teaching me through Scripture is_____

_____.

The Spirit makes me realize through the Word that I am wrong when _____

_____.

The Spirit is straightening me out through the Word so _____

_____.

The Spirit is preparing me through the Word to_____

_____.

The good things the Spirit is equipping me to do through the Word are_____

_____.

Ask Yourself . . .

❖ How often are you studying and reading the Word weekly?

❖ What is the Spirit saying to you through the Word now?

> _Write a prayer thanking the Holy Spirit for the inspired Word of God in your life:_

_____

_____

_____

_____

_____

*B*ut one who prophesies is helping others grow in the Lord, encouraging and comforting them *(1 Cor. 14:3).*

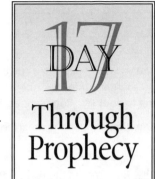

DAY 17
Through Prophecy

The Holy Spirit gives gifts to the body of Christ to help the entire church (1 Cor. 12:7). Some of His gifts are revelational such as prophecy, tongues, the interpretation of tongues, wisdom, and knowledge. Each of these gifts ministers encouragement and edification to the body of Christ.

The Holy Spirit uses people to speak prophetically for the encouragement and comfort of others. He wants to use you to prophesy into the lives of those who are hurting. Too often prophecy is misunderstood as only rebuking words of correction from God. But at its core, prophecy speaks forth God's truth in love. And whenever truth is spoken, people are set free and surrounded in the liberty of the Spirit.

2 Corinthians 1:3–7 describes God's comfort in detail for us. Read this passage, then fill in the blanks:

God's Comfort . . .

_____ is the source of all comfort.

God _____us in time of sorrow.

His comfort empowers us to comfort_____.

The more we suffer for Christ, the more Christ_____us.

As we share in suffering, we share in _____.

Prophecy afflicts those in worldly comfort and comforts those afflicted by the world. So when prophecy really stings is when we have become so acquainted with sin that any word of holiness affects us like alcohol on an open wound. But the comfort of prophecy comes in knowing that the Spirit's voice always brings healing and restoration when we hear Him obediently.

Describe a time when God's Word was spoken forth to you in a way that stung at first, but later gave great comfort:

_____

_____

_____

> *When the Holy Spirit speaks prophetically, everything His voice reveals will agree completely with the Word of God.*

Any prophetic utterance that doesn't build up, doesn't line up with the Word of God, and disrupts the body of Christ, doesn't come from God. Read 1 John 4:1–6 then with one sentence describe how you would know if a prophecy was false:

A prophecy is false when _____

_____.

Prophecy encourages us to accept and love one another as Christ loves and accepts us (1 Cor. 14:3). If prophecy becomes critical, judgmental and self-righteous, human words have replaced the Spirit's voice.

Ask Yourself . . .

❖ How is God's prophetic word encouraging you in the body of Christ?

❖ How is the Holy Spirit prophetically speaking through you to encourage and comfort others?

> *Write a prayer asking the Holy Spirit to use you to prophesy His words of comfort and encouragement to others:*

_____

_____

_____

_____

_____

*T*o one person the Spirit gives the ability to give wise advice (1 Cor. 12:8).

Through Wisdom

Wisdom is God's supernatural ability to see all of life from His perspective. It is not human or worldly. Wisdom asks, "What does God want, and what is He doing in this situation?"

So the Holy Spirit gifts certain people in the body of Christ to speak God's wisdom into people's lives. They wisely apply God's Word to life's problems giving His understanding and insight in wise answers.

If you desire to hear the Spirit's voice, listen to His wisdom as shared by those who know and correctly apply His Word. Survey what godly wisdom is in the following Scriptures, then jot down how they describe it:

Proverbs 1:7 _____

Proverbs 2:6 _____

Proverbs 2:12 _____

Proverbs 3:13–20 _____

Proverbs 8:12–36 _____

1 Corinthians 1:18–31 _____

James 1:5–8 _____

When the Holy Spirit uses someone to speak His Wisdom into your life, certain life-giving things will happen:

1. You will hear the Word clearly. Deafness to the Word will be healed.
2. You will understand the Word clearly. Confusion will be broken.
3. You will apply the Word correctly. Sinful habits will be replaced by righteous actions.
4. You will obey the Word willingly. Your rebellion and resistance to the Word will cease.

Are you having difficulty hearing the Spirit's voice of wisdom in your life? If you are, then ask for wisdom (James 1).

> *The Holy Spirit will use other believers to speak the wisdom of God's Word into your life.*

Below are some of the many ways you may hear the Holy Spirit speak a word of wisdom into your life. Check some that you have heard:

❏ Through reading and studying the Word.

❏ Through another person speaking His wisdom into your life.

❏ Through reading a Christian book or devotional.

❏ Through preaching or teaching.

❏ Through_____

The Holy Spirit will bring someone into your life when you need godly wisdom. Are you ready to listen to His voice of wisdom or are you too proud to listen and receive?

Ask Yourself . . .

❖ Are you willing to receive godly wisdom and advice from another Christian?

❖ When you need godly wisdom, will you ask the Spirit for wisdom?

Write a prayer asking the Holy Spirit to fill you with wisdom; to use you to speak wisdom to others; and to bring others with the gift of wisdom into your life and church:

_____

_____

_____

_____

_____

*T*o one person the Spirit gives the ability to give wise advise; to another he gives the gift of special knowledge (1 Cor. 12:8).

Through Knowledge

The Holy Spirit often speaks through others with the gift of special knowledge. They have an insight of us and our circumstances that reveal how God is at work in our lives.

In Acts 5, Ananias and Sapphira had sinned against God in their hearts. The knowledge of that sin was revealed to Peter. But when the Holy Spirit spoke through Peter to them, they chose to deny their sin and lie, rather than to repent. The Spirit's word was given to help, but Ananias and Sapphira rebelled against God's help and suffered the consequences instead.

If a truthful word of knowledge revealed your sin, how would you respond? Put an *x* on the line that marks your response:

Fear God	Fearing what others might think of me
Ready to repent	Ready to deny
Grateful to know my sin	Angry at the one who has the word of knowledge
Will obey no matter what the cost	Unwilling to obey

> *When the Holy Spirit reveals a knowledge about us and our situations to others, it is not to embarrass or expose us. Rather, it is to help us make right decisions and avoid tragic failures.*

At times, we desperately want a word of knowledge in our lives so we can know and understand what God is doing in and through us. But God's timing is so important. He could give us a word immediately or He could chose to be silent to have us wait for His own maturing reasons.

Why do we at times have to wait on a word of knowledge from His Spirit? Here are some reasons. Circle every one you have encountered in your spiritual walk:

Waiting will build our faith and patience.

God's perfect timing is not now, but later.

We are not yet ready and prepared to receive His word to us.

We are ready for the word but significant others in our lives aren't ready.

Unconfessed sin in our lives keeps us from hearing God's word.

His word goes against our desires, so we resist it.

Ask Yourself . . .

❖ When the Spirit wishes to speak a word of knowledge through you to another person are you willing?

❖ How ready are you to receive the next word that the Spirit has for you?

Write a prayer thanking the Holy Spirit for the words of knowledge He has given through, and to you:

_____

_____

_____

_____

_____

*S*till another person is given the ability to speak in unknown languages [or in tongues] (1 Cor. 12:10).

The Holy Spirit may speak through us with tongues to:

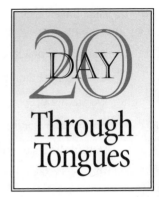

DAY 20
Through Tongues

❖ Lead the lost to Christ (Acts 2).
❖ Confirm His presence, salvation, and power (Acts 10–11).
❖ Speak prophetically to the body of Christ (1 Cor. 14).
❖ Pray through us (Rom. 8:26, 27; Jude 20).

Encountering the voice of the Spirit through tongues for the first time may thrill some, and shock others. But the Holy Spirit desires to minister through this gift regardless of how some might ridicule or reject it.

Those in Jerusalem during Pentecost in Acts 2 responded to the voice of the Spirit through tongues in various ways. Read the following verses then jot down their different responses:

Acts 2:4 _____

Acts 2:5–6 _____

Acts 2:7–8 _____

Acts 2:11 _____

Acts 2:12 _____

Acts 2:13 _____

Acts 2:41–42 _____

When the Holy Spirit speaks through His gift of tongues, what is your response? Circle the words that best describe how you respond to this vocal gift:

Joyfully	Cautiously	Excited
Confused	Perplexed	Uncomfortable
Expectantly	Obediently	Humbly
Proud	Other: _____	

> *When we respond openly to the Spirit's voice through tongues, we are enabled to pray, worship, and witness with a new boldness and power.*

This is what happened in the early church with the disciples, and the same encounter with the Holy Spirit can happen with us as well.

Are you willing to receive the gift of tongues if the Spirit so desires to speak through you? If you have received the gift of tongues, describe one way the Spirit has spoken to, or through you, with this gift:

_____

_____

If you haven't received the gift of tongues, describe how you feel about receiving this vocal spiritual gift:

_____

_____

Ask Yourself . . .

❖ How is the Holy Spirit speaking to, and through you, with the gift of tongues?

❖ If the Holy Spirit spoke through you in tongues to those around you, how do you think they would respond?

> *Write a prayer asking the Holy Spirit to fill you with His grace and ability to speak in other tongues (Luke 24:49; Acts 1:4, 5; 2:1–4). If you have already received this special gift, pray as the Spirit would lead now for five or ten minutes (1 Cor. 14:2, 4).*

_____

_____

_____

_____

*S*till another person is given the ability to speak in unknown languages [or in tongues], and another is given the ability to interpret what is being said (1 Cor. 12:10).

The voice of the Holy Spirit not only speaks in other tongues, He also gives the interpretation of what He has said.

DAY 21

Through Interpretation of Tongues

Understanding the Spirit's voice doesn't come from education, experience or enlightenment. Understanding comes from the Spirit.

"We speak words given to us by the Spirit, using the Spirit's words to explain spiritual truths" (1 Cor. 2:13).

To understand the voice of the Spirit, we must intimately know His voice. But how can we know it? Jesus explained it this way, "I am the good shepherd; I know my own sheep, and they know me, just as my Father knows me and I know the Father. And I lay down my life for the sheep. I have other sheep, too, that are not in this sheepfold. I must bring them also, and they will listen to my voice; and there will be one flock with one shepherd" (John 10:14–16).

When the Spirit speaks in His spiritual language of tongues, only the Spirit can rightly interpret. Have you encountered the Spirit's voice in this way? Describe a time when you heard both the unknown tongues of the Spirit and His accompanying interpretation:

_____

_____

Without interpretation, tongues are meaningless to the body because only the one speaking is strengthened (1 Cor. 14:4). But when tongues are interpreted, the whole body is blessed. So Paul teaches us how we are to handle these two vocal gifts. Read 1 Corinthians 14 then answer these questions:

Who does Paul wish would speak in tongues (14:5)?_____

_____.

Without interpretation who benefits from tongues (14:4)?_____

_____.

If someone speaks in tongues, what then should we pray for (14:13–14)?_____

_____.

For whom are tongues a sign (14:22)? _____

_____.

How will unbelievers respond to tongues (14:22–25)? _____

_____.

What does Paul say should be permitted and how should worship be conducted (14:39–40)? _____

_____.

When you experience the Spirit's voice through other tongues, also seek His voice to interpret. Because His interpretation will conform to God's Word and will strengthen, correct, build up, and minister to your deepest needs (1 Cor. 14:2, 4).

Ask Yourself . . .

❖ What is the Holy Spirit's voice interpreting for your life?

❖ When you hear tongues, will you ask the Spirit to give to you the interpretation of what you hear?

Write a prayer asking the Holy Spirit to interpret His voice for you:

_____

_____

_____

_____

_____

*T*hen after I have poured out my rains again, I
will pour out my Spirit upon all people. Your
sons and daughters will prophesy. Your old men
will dream dreams. Your young men will see visions
(Joel 2:28).

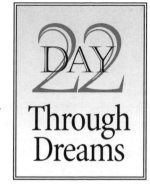

DAY 22
Through Dreams

The Spirit speaks to us through dreams. In a dream,
we may receive a spiritual scenario and hear His
voice. So the Spirit also gives the interpretation to
our dreams, because not all dreams are from God.

> *The Spirit of God sometimes speaks through dreams so He can reveal*
> *His Word to us in such a way that we are consumed with His revelation.*

Since we are asleep, God's dreams can come to us without being altered or
interpreted by our rational thoughts. In others words, the Spirit can speak
directly to our spirit without interference or interruption.

How the Spirit speaks in dreams is illustrated in two biblical stories. The first is
Jacob's dream at Bethel. Read Genesis 28:10–22. Below are some of the truths
we can learn about this spiritual stream of revelation. Write the verse from
Genesis 28 next to the appropriate truth.

Dreams from the Holy Spirit are . . .

1. Given as the recipient sleeps.   _____

2. Inspired by God.   _____

3. Can contain an allegorical scene from God.   _____

4. Interpreted by God.   _____

5. Confirm God's Word.   _____

Remember, not every dream is from God's Spirit. But we know that a dream is
from God when all of the above criteria are met.

Now let's explore a second dream. Read Genesis 41:1–36 then complete the
following questions:

Who interprets dreams (vs. 16)? _____

_____.

The interpretation of dreams correctly gives confirmation of what (vs. 38)?

_____

_____.

When the Holy Spirit chooses to give you a dream and interprets its for you, will you be prepared to receive? Below are some specific steps and attitudes you can take to be prepared for this revelational stream. Check all that you have done in preparation:

      ❑ Pray for the Spirit to speak to you in dreams.

      ❑ Read the Word, pray, and worship seeking God before you sleep.

      ❑ Have pencil and paper ready to write down His dream and inter-
         pretation.

      ❑ If the interpretation doesn't come within the dream, have other
         believers willing to pray with you for an interpretation.

      ❑ Know and understand the Word so well that you can test every
         dream received by the Word of God.

Remember, if you spend your time before sleep taking in garbage from the world through television, radio, or the print media, your dreams will be littered with trash. So be filled throughout each day until you go to sleep with the song of the Lord, prayer, Scripture, and the Holy Spirit. To dream the Spirit's dreams invites the Spirit's presence.

Ask Yourself . . .

❖ In what ways does the Word and the Holy Spirit's presence fill you each day?

❖ What dream(s) has the Spirit given you that needs your action and obedience?

Write a prayer asking God's Spirit to speak to you through spiritual dreams:

_____

_____

_____

*I*n the last days," God said, "I will pour out my Spirit upon all people. Your sons and daughters will prophesy, your young men will see visions, and your old men will dream dreams." *(Acts 2:17)*

Visions through which the Spirit speaks bring hope and life to God's people. The Holy Spirit inspired visions to give fresh revelation to His prophets and servants through Scripture.

Here are some Scriptures describing how visions came to God's people. Read each passage, then jot down what it reveals about this prophetic stream:

Genesis 15:1–6 _____

Numbers 12:6, 24:16–17 _____

Isaiah 6:1–4 _____

Isaiah 21:2 _____

Lamentations 2:9 _____

Ezekiel 1:1–2:1, 3:23 _____

Daniel 1:17, 7:13–28 _____

Amos 7:1–7, 8:1, 9:1 _____

Luke 1:22 _____

John 12:41 _____

Acts 9:10, 10:3–20 _____

Acts 18:9–10 _____

2 Cor. 12:1 _____

Revelation 1:10–20, 4:2, 17:3, 21:10 _____

The Holy Spirit speaks to His people through dreams and visions. Dreams come as we sleep, while visions come while asleep or awake (Dan. 7:1). We can dialogue with the Spirit during a vision as Abraham did (Gen. 15). And visions may reveal the future, including the awesome judgment of God. But there will also be those who claim to have visions who are deceivers and should not be believed (2 Thess. 2:1–3).

In Acts 9, we read one of the most dramatic accounts of a vision in the Bible. Saul of Tarsus had a dramatic vision of the Lord and was changed on the road to Damascus. Read Acts 9, then survey what can be learned about visions from this account. Circle each truth you have encountered in your life regarding visions from God.

God speaks directly to us through visions.

Visions speak conviction and correction into our lives.

Visions may reveal what we must do to follow Christ.

We can talk with God in a vision.

His voice interprets the meaning of what is revealed in a vision.

When the Lord commands something in a vision, we are to obey.

Visions can overcome our fears and reluctance to obey God.

As with dreams, test a vision you receive by the Word of God, by the witness of the Holy Spirit within you, and with the fellowship of believers.

> *Visions don't verify the spiritual maturity of a person,*
> *only their willingness to be open to His voice.*

Continual openness to the voice of the Spirit through dreams and visions will give direction and guidance to us as we walk in the Spirit.

Ask Yourself . . .

❖ Are you open to hearing from God's Spirit through visions?

❖ Have you obeyed what He has commanded you to do in the past through visions?

Write a prayer asking the Holy Spirit to speak to you through visions:

_____

_____

_____

_____

*T*hey made their hearts as hard as stone, so they could not hear the law or the messages that the Lord Almighty had sent them by his Spirit through the earlier prophets (Zech. 7:12).

Tender, broken, and contrite hearts are ready to listen and to obey. But hardened, calloused hearts are deaf to Him night and day. The condition of our hearts determines our receptivity to the Spirit's voice.

What is the condition of your heart? Is your heart tender enough to hear the Spirit's voice? Read the following scriptures that speak about the heart, then write on the heart below all the qualities we need to be open to the Spirit: [Deut. 6:5; 1 Sam. 12:20; Ps. 9:1, 51:6–17, 61:1–3, 66:18, 86:11–12; Ezek. 18:31; Acts 2:26]

_____   _____

_____   _____

_____   _____

_____   _____

What hardens a heart toward God (Ex. 8:19)? If we are to hear the Spirit's voice, we can't harden our hearts toward Him. "Today you must listen to his voice. Don't harden your hearts against him" (Heb. 4:7). But many things can callous us to keep us from hearing the messages of God's Spirit that He wants us to hear. Here are some of those things. Check any that apply to you:

❑ Prayerlessness.

❑ Love grown cold.

❑ Rebellion.

❑ Pride.

❑ Unconfessed sin.

❑ Unbelief.

❑ Lack of worship and praise.

❑ Forsaking gathering together in Christian fellowship.

❑ Other: _____

> *Only a broken and contrite heart can hear the Spirit's messages.*

If you haven't heard from the Spirit lately, check the condition of your heart, then repent of any hardness you may find there.

Ask Yourself . . .

❖ Are you staying continually in the Lord's presence by keeping your heart humbled and tender toward Him?

❖ What messages have you heard from the Spirit in your heart that still need to be obeyed?

Write a prayer of repentance so your heart may be more tender toward God:

_____

_____

_____

_____

_____

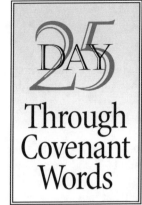

A nd this is my covenant with them," says the Lord. "My Spirit will not leave them, and neither will these words I have given you. They will be on your lips and on the lips of your children and your children's children forever. I, the Lord, have spoken!" (Isa. 59:21).

God cuts His covenant (*beriyth*) with His people. A covenant is a promise made by God to His people involving human responsibilities of reciprocation. Men and women receive God's covenant word that promises His Spirit will not leave us and that it will be on our lips and the lips of our future generations. But it's up to us to obey His instructions, and pass them along.

> *Each time the Spirit speaks God's covenant words through us, we declare in time and space the promises of God for ourselves and future generations.*

The covenants that God makes with His people are filled with blessing and commands for obedience.

The covenant word from God's Spirit will . . .

- ❖ Remind us of our relationship with God.
- ❖ Recall to our memory all the mighty things He has done for us.
- ❖ Speak life and Spirit into our children. "And the very words I have spoken to you are spirit and life" (John 6:63).
- ❖ Declare to the world and the enemy that we are standing firm in God's covenant promises.

Below are three examples of covenant words the Spirit has sealed in the Word and put on our lips for power and life. Read each covenant out loud. Teach them to your children and let the Spirit speak His covenant words through you.

> *I will bless you and make you famous,*
> *And I will make you a blessing to others.*
> *I will bless those who bless you*
> *And curse those who curse you.*
> *All the families of the earth will be blessed through you.*
> *—Abrahamic covenant, Genesis 12:2–3*

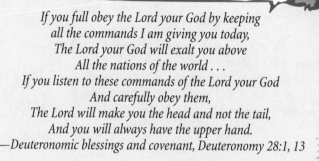

If you full obey the Lord your God by keeping
all the commands I am giving you today,
The Lord your God will exalt you above
All the nations of the world . . .
If you listen to these commands of the Lord your God
And carefully obey them,
The Lord will make you the head and not the tail,
And you will always have the upper hand.
—Deuteronomic blessings and covenant, Deuteronomy 28:1, 13

This is my body which is given for you.
Do this in remembrance of me [Jesus].
This cup is the new covenant between God and you,
Sealed by the shedding of blood.
Do this in remembrance of me as often as you drink it.
—New Covenant, 1 Corinthians 11:24–25

Decide to speak these covenant words daily. And as you speak them, let the Holy Spirit confirm them in your mind and hide them in your heart.

Ask Yourself . . .

❖ Are you mindful daily of the covenant you have in Christ that has been sealed in His blood by the Holy Spirit?

❖ What other covenant words does the Spirit speak to you from the Word every day?

Write a prayer asking God's Spirit to bring to your memory His covenant with you in Christ every day:

_____

_____

_____

*B*ut as for me, I am filled with power and the Spirit of the Lord. I am filled with justice and might, fearlessly pointing out Israel's sin and rebellion (Micah 3:8).

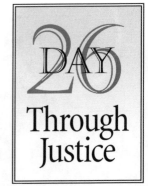

The Spirit's voice is not always gentle and tender. The thunder of His prophetic righteousness can ring out from His prophets to expose sin and rebellion, because the Holy Spirit also speaks with a mighty voice of justice. He powerfully uses His servants and prophets to declare God's righteous judgment on sin.

When was the last time you heard the Spirit's voice declaring God's righteousness, holiness, and justice, on the following issues? Put an *x* on the lines that apply:

The Spirit's prophetic judgment and justice pointing out the sins of . . .

Governmental corruption
_____
Heard recently   Not heard

The plight of the poor
_____
Heard recently   Not heard

Abortion
_____
Heard recently   Not heard

The needs of the homeless
_____
Heard recently   Not heard

Injustice in the courts
_____
Heard recently   Not heard

Racial prejudice
_____
Heard recently   Not heard

Immorality
_____
Heard recently   Not heard

Materialism
_____
Heard recently   Not heard

God's Spirit roars out His displeasure with cultural, corporate, and individual sins. He also despises empty ritual and religious traditions. Read Amos 5, then list five things the Spirit's voice will judge that Israel was guilty of that apply to our culture today.

1. _____

2. _____

3. _____

4. _____

5. _____

> *If you are open to hearing the Spirit's voice, prepare yourself to hear and obey when He requires you to speak His justice.*

Ask Yourself . . .

❖ Are you listening to the Holy Spirit speak justice?

❖ What does He wish to speak through you?

> *Write a prayer asking the Spirit to reveal where He desires righteousness and justice in those you know and in our nation. Then acknowledge your obedience to be His "prophet" in the land:*

_____

_____

_____

_____

_____

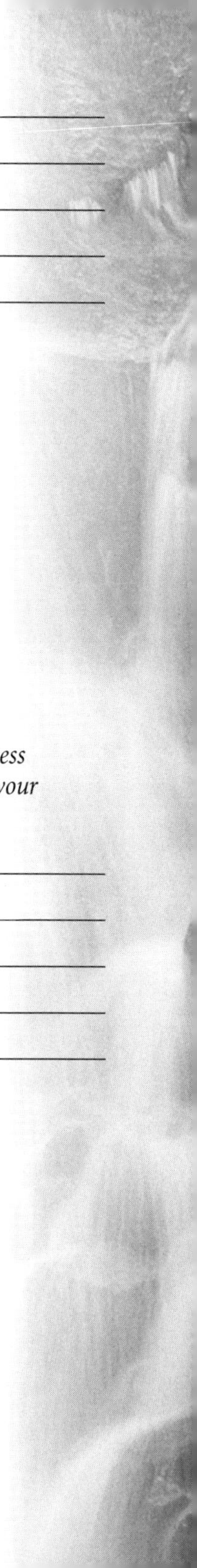

*W*hen you are arrested, don't worry about what to say in your defense, because you will be given the right words at the right time. For it won't be you doing the talking—it will be the Spirit of your Father speaking through you (Matt. 10:20).

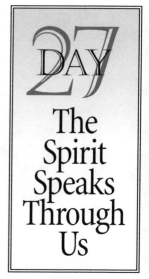

DAY 27

The Spirit Speaks Through Us

How exciting it is to know that the Holy Spirit can and will speak through us to give a witness of His presence. But we must always be ready to give an answer (speak His words) for the hope of Christ within us (1 Peter 3:15).

We may not always know how to respond. But the Holy Spirit does, because He knows the hearts of those who question us. So He also always knows the right kind of answer to give, which will please the Father. Read the following promises about how the Spirit will speak through us, then write down how and when the Spirit speaks through us:

Isaiah 50:4 _____

2 Samuel 23:2 _____

Matthew 10:19–20 _____

Luke 12:11–12 _____

Luke 21:14–15 _____

John 3:27 _____

Acts 4:8 _____

1 Corinthians 2:13 _____

Ephesians 3:5–6:19–20 _____

James 1:5 _____

1 Peter 1:12 _____

Now consider the situations in which you most need the Spirit's voice to speak through you. Below is a list of some of those possible situations. Rank in order from 1 (most needful for the Spirit to speak through me), to 7 (least needful):

_____ When I get angry with others.

_____ When I need to share deep feelings.

_____ When I witness to someone who is lost.

_____ When I am explaining the person and work of the Holy Spirit to someone who believes all spiritual gifts have ceased.

_____ When I am confessing my sins.

_____ When I am worshiping.

_____ When I am praying.

_____ Other:_____

Our tongues need to speak life—not death (Prov. 18:21).

> *When the Holy Spirit speaks through us, we can be assured His living water flows from us to others.*

So, we need to allow the Spirit in all situations to speak through us. Because without His words, our words are meaningless.

Ask Yourself . . .

❖ The next time you speak, will you ask yourself, "Are my words from the Spirit or from my flesh?"

❖ Into whose life do you most need to speak the Spirit's words right now?

Write a prayer asking the Holy Spirit to take control of your tongue:

_____

_____

_____

_____

_____

*B*ut if I am casting out demons by the Spirit of God, then the Kingdom of God has arrived among you (Matt. 12:28).

When demons encounter the Holy Spirit in us, they must flee. Why? "Because the Spirit who lives in you is greater than the spirit who lives in the world" (1 John 4:4). We have the right, the authority, and the power in the Holy Spirit to cast out demons in Jesus' name (Mark 16:17). So we have nothing to fear when confronting demons.

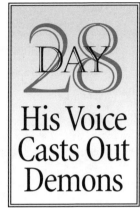

Day 28
His Voice Casts Out Demons

But exorcism doesn't just happen because we recite a formula with Jesus' name. The power and Spirit of Jesus Christ must fully indwell us if demons are to flee. And we must speak with the Spirit's voice in Christ's authority, not with our own.

Read Acts 19:8–20, then summarize what happened to those who tried to speak to demons without the powerful voice of the Holy Spirit:

_____

_____

_____

We can learn how the Spirit casts out demons when we study the ministry of Jesus. Jesus was the *anointed One.* He was anointed with the power of the Holy Spirit to heal, deliver, save, and cast out demons. Read how Jesus spoke to demons in the power of the Holy Spirit in the following scriptures, then jot down what He did and taught:

Matthew 12:22–37 _____

Mark 5:1–20 _____

Mark 7:24–30 _____

Mark 9:14–29 _____

Luke 9:37–43 _____

Luke 11:14–28 _____

When confronted with demonic power, take heart. You're not powerless. The same Holy Spirit that indwelt Jesus and raised Him from the dead also indwells and empowers you. So speak with the Spirit's voice to anything that is unclean and defiled spiritually, and it must leave in the name of Jesus.

> *Because the power of the Holy Spirit indwells you, you have nothing to fear from demons.*

Demons can't possess you. They can only harass or oppress you if you let them through an open door of unconfessed sin or rebellion against God. Have you opened the door to demonic attack? The following things can provide Satan an easy open door. Circle any you may have opened:

The Occult	Immorality	Addiction
Abuse	Unconfessed sin	Pride
Rebellion	Hate and bitterness	Prayerlessness

Now seek God's love and power to close any open doors. Don't give Satan a demonic foothold in your life. Walk in the power of the Spirit and no evil thing can touch you.

Ask Yourself . . .

❖ Do you fear the demonic? If so, repent and confess your true identity in Jesus to close the door(s).

❖ Will you allow the Holy Spirit in you to speak in Jesus' name to demons and cast them out?

Write a prayer asking the Holy Spirit to fill you with power and boldness to be free from demonic harrassment and to confront and cast out any demon you meet in Jesus' name:

_____

_____

_____

_____

_____

*A*ll around him was a glowing halo, like a rainbow shining through the clouds. This was the way the glory of the Lord appeared to me. When I saw it, I fell face down in the dust, and I heard someone's voice speaking to me. "Stand up, son of man," said the voice. "I want to speak with you." The Spirit came into me as he spoke and set me on my feet. I listened carefully to His words (Ezek. 1:28–2:2).

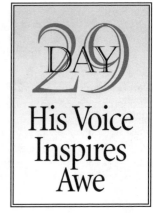

DAY 29
His Voice Inspires Awe

Can you imagine being Ezekiel? Suddenly you have a vision of the Lord in His glory. This is not a casual meeting. It is an encounter! Then all you can do is fall to your face. The fear of God and awe fill your being and press you to the floor! You are enveloped in the presence, power, and voice of our living God! Wow!

Ezekiel was graced with an unusual prophetic vision. Though the Spirit usually speaks in less dramatic ways, maybe you have had such an encounter, because He does physically manifest Himself. When you hear the voice of the Spirit and encounter His presence, what response fills your being? Circle all that apply:

Awe	Surprise	Excitement
Joy	Fear	Mystery
Hope	Expectancy	Other:_____

In Ezekiel's instance, he fell on his face before the presence of the Lord. Then as the Spirit spoke, Ezekiel was lifted up and put on His feet. Imagine the awesome power the prophet must have experienced as God's Spirit spoke and presenced with him. When we physically encounter the Spirit we may tremble, shake, fall, or simply freeze in place. Have you experienced the presence of His Spirit in such a dynamic physical way? Complete these sentences:

When I encounter the Holy Spirit's presence and voice . . .

I feel _____

_____

I think _____

_____

I physically _____

_____

I spiritually _____

_____ .

The Holy Spirit speaks to us continually through various means. Both His sovereignty, and our receptivity, play a role in how He speaks. He knows our every feeling and response. So the Spirit may approach us in a way that will command our attention and awe. But regardless of how He approaches us, the Spirit's voice will always direct us to toward the will of God. His presence fills us with love and awe for the Father. And His power enables us to respond in holy obedience to His powerful voice.

> *While we don't fear God's awesome presence or His voice, we respond with awe in reverential fear.*

Like Ezekiel, we are completely awestruck and humbled in His presence. When He speaks, we worship. When He directs, we obey. When He sends, we go.

Ask Yourself . . .

❖ How do you discipline yourself moment by moment to hear His voice?

❖ When you hear His voice, what is your immediate response?

Write a prayer thanking the Holy Spirit for the grace and mercy He demonstrates each time He speaks to you:

_____

_____

_____

_____

_____

It is the Spirit who gives eternal life. Human effort accomplishes nothing. And the very words I have spoken to you are spirit and life (John 6:63).

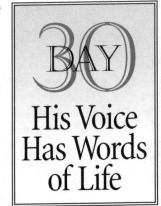

DAY 30

His Voice Has Words of Life

The Father wills. The Son speaks. And the Spirit imparts the voice of His Word into our hearts. We hear and understand the things of the Spirit by the Spirit (1 Cor. 2).

In this devotional study, we have explored and discovered how the Holy Spirit speaks and the means He uses to communicate God's Word to us. We have also discovered the awesome power of His voice.

> *When Jesus speaks His Word of life to us, the Spirit of God empowers us to hear and obey His truth.*

As exciting as it is to hear the Spirit's voice, we must move beyond excitement to obedience. "Anyone who is willing to hear should listen to the Spirit and understand what the Spirit is saying to the churches" (Rev. 3:6). The message coming from the Spirit is not just to be listened to, it is to be obeyed. "And remember, it is a message to obey, not just to listen to. If you don't obey, you are only fooling yourself" (James 1:22).

So take a moment now to summarize some of what you have learned by completing the following sentences:

What impresses me most about the Spirit's voice is_____
_____.

I hear the Spirit's voice when _____
_____.

The most exciting thing I have learned about the Spirit's voice is_____
_____.

To hear His voice more clearly, I must _____
_____.

The gift He uses in me to speak to others is_____
_____.

One thing I must do to obey His voice is _____
_____.

I love to hear the Spirit's voice when _____
_____.

Ask Yourself . . .

❖ Is anything keeping you from hearing the Holy Spirit's voice constantly?

❖ Are you willing to obey the Spirit's voice whenever He speaks?

Write a prayer asking God's Spirit to never stop speaking to your life:

_____

_____

_____

_____

_____

You can continue your encounters with the Holy Spirit by using the other devotional study guides listed at the end of this booklet, and by using the companion *Holy Spirit Encounter Bible.*

Leader's Guide

For Group Sessions

This devotional study is an excellent resource for group study including such settings as:

❖ Sunday school classes and other church classes
❖ Prayer groups
❖ Bible study groups
❖ Ministries involving small groups, home groups, and accountability groups
❖ Study groups for youth and adults

Before the first session:

❖ Contact everyone interested in participating in your group to inform them about the meeting time, date, and place.
❖ Make certain that everyone has a copy of *Hearing the Spirit's Voice*.
❖ Plan out all your teaching lessons before starting the first session. Also ask group members to begin their daily encounters in this guide. While each session will not strictly adhere to a seven-day schedule, group members who faithful study a devotional every day will be prepared to share in the group sessions.
❖ Pray for the Holy Spirit to guide, teach, and help each participant.
❖ Be certain the place where you meet has a chalkboard, white board, or flipchart with appropriate writing materials.

Planning the Group Sessions

1. You will have four sessions together as a group. So plan to cover at least seven days in each session.

2. In your first session, have group members find a partner with whom they will share and pray each time you meet. Keep the same pairs throughout the group sessions. See if you can randomly put pairs together—men with men, and women with women.

3. Have group and class members complete their devotional studies prior to their group sessions to enhance group sharing, study, and prayer. Begin each session with prayer.

4. Either the group leader or selected members should read the key Scriptures from each of the seven daily devotionals you will be studying in the session.

5. As the leader, you should decide which exercises and questions are to be covered prior to each session.

6. Also decide which exercises and sessions will be most appropriate to share with the group as a whole, or in pairs.

7. Decide which prayer(s) from the seven devotionals you will want the pairs to pray with one another.

8. Close each session by giving every group member the opportunity to share with the group how he or she encountered the Holy Spirit during the previous week. Then lead the group in prayer or have group members pray aloud in a prayer circle as you close the session.

9. You will have nine days of devotionals to study in the last session. So, use the last day as an in-depth sharing time in pairs. Invite every group member to share the most important thing they learned about the Holy Spirit during this study and how their relationship with the Spirit was deepened because of it. Close with prayers of praise and thanksgiving.

10. Remember to allow each person the freedom "not to share" with their prayer partner or in public if they are uncomfortable with it.

11. Always start and end each group session on time and seek to keep them no longer than ninety minutes.

12. Finally, be careful. This is not a therapy group. Group members who seek to dominate group discussions with their own problems or questions should be ministered to by the group leader or pastor one-on-one outside of the group session.

Titles in the Holy Spirit Encounter Guide Series

Additional Notes

Additional Notes

Additional Notes

Additional Notes

Additional Notes

Additional Notes

Additional Notes

Additional Notes

Additional Notes

Additional Notes